For Allana

Content

Chapter 1

What Is Social Contract Theory?

If you've ever discussed politics at a level more in-depth than red vs blue, someone has probably brought up Social Contract Theory. This topic is filled with convoluted and fuzzy thinking. In this book, I intend to help clear things up as well as show why at best, we should be highly skeptical of any variant of Social Contract Theory

For this book, what I mean by Social Contract Theory is a concept that attempts to explain why states (synonymous with what most people refer to as the government) have the authority to rule. In other words, it addresses the question of why it is O.K. for state agents to do things to civilians which civilians are typically not allowed to do to others. Additionally, Social Contract Theory tries to show why citizens of a nation-state should be obligated to obey the rules which are set forth.

You might ask: "Why does Social Contract Theory matter?" As I have mentioned, the state and/or state agents do things to people most of us would consider illegitimate if done by a non-state agent or entity. They can tax, imprison, conscript, fine, enforce myriad laws and in general, order others around. How we view the nature of the state is greatly impacted by whether or not there is a convincing and coherent argument that explains why it has these privileges. Without a robust theory, law enforcement looks more like arbitrary violence, conscription starts to look similar to slavery, and taxes become comparable to robbery. Understanding whether or not these theories have merit informs our broader perspective on politics.

In my many political discussions, I have encountered a large number of justifications for state authority. Given the nature of many of these arguments, the fact that they are so varied presents a problem for adherents of Social Contract Theory. If you ask 10 people why states have the authority to make and enforce the law, you will probably get 10 different answers (or more). But as the name implies, many versions of Social Contract Theory center around the idea that there is some sort of agreement between the state and its citizens, or between all members of society. So, the fact that people have heterogeneous ideas of what the social contract is and the obligations it entails, makes a claim about some "agreement" rather dubious. If there truly was an agreement about such a crucial issue, wouldn't we all know what it was? Sure, there could be some minor differences in interpretation, but common responses range from "we delegated politicians to rule over us" or "we all owe something to each other" or "you benefit from state services, so you are obligated to obey." to "the state protects your rights in exchange for your obedience" and even "you consented to the social contract by living here." All imply some agreement or common understanding of obligations or means of acquiring obligations, yet all these examples describe a social contract that is somewhat different. Clearly, we can see there is no common understanding.

This lack of consensus is merely a glimpse into the difficulties any theory must overcome. Throughout the rest of the book, I will describe all of the justifications for state authority and versions of Social Contract Theory that I have encountered and present my arguments for why they fail.

Chapter 2

"If You Don't Like It, Leave!"

If you've ever questioned why the state has the authority to do something or even wondered aloud whether the status quo is the best that it could be, it's likely someone has told you some variant of "If you don't like it, leave!" This phrase is less an argument than it is an emotional outburst. It's usually uttered when someone wants to cover their ears and shut down the discussion. If we give the benefit of the doubt, however, there is a semblance of an argument behind this phrase.

First of all, no, many people cannot easily leave. Some are too poor, too old, too young, or have responsibilities or dependents which demand their presence. In the United States, the fee for renouncing[1] your citizenship is over $2,300. And simply leaving the U.S. does not get the IRS off your back. You are still required[2] to pay taxes regardless of where you live. Right off the bat, this argument seems to only apply to the relatively well-off who are capable of moving long distances, and even that does not remove the imposed taxes and fees. Additionally, it's worth noting those who do wish to leave are concerned with leaving the political system, not a geographic area. As far as I know, there is only one nation-state on earth that allows people to leave the political apparatus — Liechtenstein.[3] And even there, it is not permitted at the individual level, but rather for municipalities. Strictly speaking, leaving only the political system of nearly every current state, is not allowed by that state.

If the concern is whether states have legitimate authority, a suggestion to move to another nation-state fails to address the problem. Nearly all of the planet is controlled by states. Even Antarctica[4] is divided by territorial claims of multiple countries. So the argument transforms into "if you don't like it, move to the middle of the ocean or the moon!" This response fails to account for non-coastal regions of the ocean being regulated by the United Nations Convention on the Law of the Sea.[5] "Don't like it, leave" can make sense in some contexts, like when alternatives are plentiful and reasonably attainable. But when the only option to avoid being subject to the authority of a state is to leave the planet, this response loses any persuasiveness it might have had.

"Don't like it, leave." could be interpreted in a few different ways. Perhaps the phrase implies that since you are within the jurisdiction of a state, you are obligated to obey its rules. This is a form of circular reasoning. It begs the question. Jurisdiction, after all, is a synonym for authority. To see the circularity more clearly, just rephrase the argument with more direct terms. For example, "The state has the authority to control you because you are in the territory which it has the authority to control." The conclusion of the argument contains its premise. Rather than proving anything, this sentence is merely a baseless assertion. For this prior argument to have merit, it must first be shown that the state's authority is justified

Alternatively, the claim could be that the state owns all of the lands within the specified borders. It should be pointed out this would negate the idea of any private property. I suspect almost everyone who thinks of it in this way hasn't thought through the logic. Many advocates of social contract theory, after all, also at least claim to support private property rights. But if the state owns the whole country, then there is no private property. Additionally, in just about every case, nation-states took control of their land through conquest. Endorsing conquest as a just form of property acquisition requires supporting mass murder, enslavement, pillaging, theft, subjugation, etc. When pressed, most people do not think these actions are a justified means of acquiring forms of property.

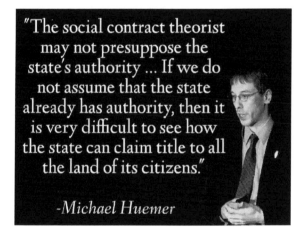

"The social contract theorist may not presuppose the state's authority ... If we do not assume that the state already has authority, then it is very difficult to see how the state can claim title to all the land of its citizens."

-Michael Huemer

Even if we could leave the claimed authority or territory of states, which is practically impossible for just about everyone, there remains the unanswered question of why a given state's authority is justified anyway. "Don't like it, leave." is a blatant attempt to avoid that very question.

Chapter 3

Implied and Explicit Consent

Going by the name, you would think Social Contract Theory involved some form of written contract—an explicit, signed agreement detailing both the obligations of citizens and the state. And frankly, given the complexity of the purported contract, characterized by the innumerable laws that citizens are expected to follow, a detailed written agreement is the only thing that could make sense.

The Constitution is sometimes proposed as that contract. The Constitution as a mutual agreement, however, has several glaring flaws. For one, it was written, signed and ratified well over 200 years ago. I know of no contract which can impose obligations on people who did not even exist at the time it was formed. Nor could our ancestors' contracts create obligations be passed on to us today. After all, that would not represent our consent, but the consent of our ancestors. Of course, this all assumes the people at the time of the ratification were asked permission to opt into the agreement. In general, they were not. There were only a few dozen people who signed it, and despite their claims of representation, they did not first gain explicit permission to represent the millions of people living in the relevant territory.

Even if we take this perverted notion of "representation" for granted, the Constitution's ratification did not rely upon freely given consent by all the states' representatives. Most notably, Rhode Island was coerced into ratification.[6] Ratification was extremely unpopular in the small state, but soon after the United States Senate passed a bill banning trade between Rhode islanders and the other states, Rhode Island ratified, and the bill was nullified. This demonstrates that failure to ratify wasn't an option that the majority of states would tolerate. This cannot represent a consensual relationship.

That there is no explicit contract is obvious to most people. As an alternative, one of the ways states are said to gain the rightful authority to rule is through implied consent. It is claimed that in some way or another, the citizenry implicitly agrees to follow laws. Do we implicitly consent to be ruled? Is there some action we take that could reasonably be construed as voluntarily agreeing to follow all forms of law which are put forth by the state? How accurate is it to say that "consent of the governed" is upheld?

Presumably, laws, regulations, and state authority, in general, applies to people of all ages. Granted, children are typically treated somewhat differently than adults before the law, but the state still exercises sovereignty. What action could a child possibly perform that would signify consent? If state authority applies to all humans, then birth would be the declaratory act of consent. But of course, birth is not even a choice. One wonders how a non-voluntary act could conceivably be taken as any form of consent.

Furthermore, we have the issue of informed consent. In no other context would we say a child, let alone a baby, could provide informed consent to enter into any complex agreement or transaction. Given the far-reaching effects of an agreement with the state to perpetually follow every rule it lays down, it may very well require the most informed consent of any interaction possible. If a child could agree to this serious of a commitment, he or she would also be capable of agreeing to any other contract. Unless supporters of the implied consent doctrine also want to endorse the idea that children are capable of consenting to things like prostitution or taking hard drugs, I would suggest they stay far away from applying it to children.

If we rule out children from the social contract, the question then becomes what specific action is taken by a maturing person that signifies consent. Simply turning 18 cannot represent consent because it is not a choice.

Some will claim that deciding to use government services is implicitly agreeing to pay for them and/or to follow their rules. Prima facie, this makes at least a little bit of sense. After all, such an arrangement resembles other interactions we regularly engage in on the market. And if driving on a road only implied agreeing to pay for a share of that road and abide by some driving rules, this wouldn't be a terrible concept. The question that arises though, is how things like drug prohibition, foreign intervention, or myriad other government actions are justified because we use state-provided services. It's difficult to see why driving on a public road, would represent implicitly consenting to a no-knock raid on your home as police search for drugs. Nor is it clear why utilizing a public library is an endorsement for intelligence agencies and the military to use your resources to intervene in nations around the world.

The fundamental problem is that government services are generally not directly connected to payment. It is common for people to be forced to pay for things they don't use (examples can include foreign intervention, corporate bailouts, foreign aid,) just as it is common to receive services without needing to pay (e.g. welfare, public housing, law enforcement).

If a state was limited to only charging for specific services rendered, and only set rules for the use of those services, then the sovereign authority of that state is no longer in question. If that is all a "state" does, it is no longer a state. It's merely another private entity engaged in the production of services.

Does the act of voting or any other form of participation in the political apparatus mean we agree to follow the rules laid down by that political body? First of all, not everyone votes. Yet, states maintain their authority over everyone regardless of their participation. If we are subjected to laws whether we supposedly opt-in via the vote or not, then clearly a vote represents nothing of the sort!

It is often claimed politicians are our representatives. But "representative" used in this context is an abuse of the term. If a politician truly represented you, you could call him up and instruct him on how to act in your place. Then if he failed to live up to your expectations, you could fire him on the spot. What, in reality, happens is politicians claim to represent hundreds, thousands, or even hundreds of thousands of people. Besides the impracticability of accurately representing the interests of so many people, there remains the objection that these people were not individually asked if they could be represented. And since a politician will assume power over everyone regardless if some citizens explicitly voted against her or didn't vote at all, a vote for the winner does not signify consent to be ruled any more than voting any other way. Unless a non-vote equals non-consent, a vote cannot equal consent.

People who make claims of being represented by politicians often ignore the fact that almost every single election an individual's vote doesn't matter. Don't misunderstand me. I am not saying votes in the aggregate do not matter. I am saying a singular vote that is cast is seldom the vote that decides which candidate wins. The only instance in which a single vote makes the difference is when a candidate wins by 1 vote. This is incredibly rare, even at the local level. In effect, this means no single individual has a say in how they are governed or who represents them (barring an extremely close race). This is actually generous. Many voters often prefer a candidate who has no chance of winning but vote for one of two candidates because they are the only ones with a realistic shot.

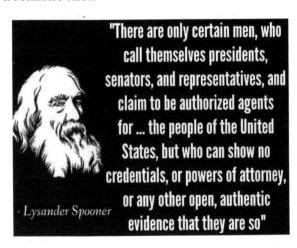

"There are only certain men, who call themselves presidents, senators, and representatives, and claim to be authorized agents for ... the people of the United States, but who can show no credentials, or powers of attorney, or any other open, authentic evidence that they are so"

- Lysander Spooner

One last implicit consent argument is that since we benefit from government services or actions, we are obligated to pay. This begs the question. Anyone who is questioning why they should be obligated to obey the state's edicts probably has serious doubts about whether the government provides a net benefit anyway. "Benefit" after all, is a subjective valuation. In my opinion, the sum result of all government actions is probably a severely negative effect for everyone outside of the very well politically connected. This would be a difficult assertion to prove one way or the other, however. So I will address this argument under the best assumptions.

Even if we grant that citizens benefit immensely from the policies of their wise overlords, that would not incur obligations on the beneficiaries. This is otherwise known as the positive externalities argument. A positive externality is when a third party benefits indirectly from the interactions of others. Imagine if every time a person experienced some sort of benefit, they could be forced to pay for it. Randomly washing a stranger's car would obligate the owner to pay up. Planting a beautiful garden in your yard could authorize you to demand payment from your neighbors for the improved view. In fact, almost every action we do could bestow a positive externality upon some lucky soul (just as it could generate a negative one). When taken to its logical conclusion, we can see the problem with this theory is that it does not rely on the consent of the beneficiary, and leads to impractical results. Which is why in every other case we require an explicit contract for services.

The fundamental problem with the above arguments is they require carving out a large exception for the state. In no other contexts do these rationalizations make sense. In short, a theory of implied consent for state authority requires us to already accept that the state has a form of authority which no other person or entity has.

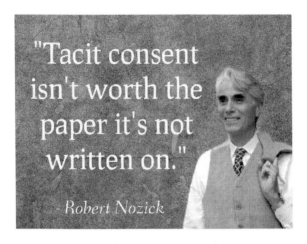

Chapter 4

The Social Contract Is Null and Void

As has been discussed in prior chapters, it is unclear how or when citizens supposedly entered into the social contract. But let us suppose they did. Let us assume citizens have agreed to obey the state's edicts in exchange for protection.

In the United States at least, such a theory does not hold up under scrutiny. The state's courts have ruled there is no such obligation for government officials. In Warren v. District of Columbia,[7] the court cited "a government and its agents are under no general duty to provide public services, such as police protection, to any particular individual citizen". Similar decisions have been reached in Hartzler v. City of San Jose,[8] Castle Rock V. Gonzales,[9] and in DeShaney v. Winnebago County Department of Social Services.[10] The latter was upheld by the U.S. Supreme Court.

In fact, in Castle Rock V. Gonzales, Justice Stevens commented that if personal security is desired it should be purchased on the market. "It is perfectly clear, on the one hand, that neither the Federal Constitution itself, nor any federal statute, granted respondent or her children any individual entitlement to police protection.

...Respondent certainly could have entered into a contract with a private security firm, obligating the firm to provide protection to the respondent's family."

Perhaps the government is only obligated to protect the public at large, as opposed to individuals? This notion was put to the test in a suit against the Broward County Sheriff's Office following the Parkland Massacre, in which multiple officers who were on the scene failed[11] to intervene. Despite the shooting taking place at a public high school filled with children and faculty, the court followed in the footsteps of past rulings and found[12] no obligations of officers to protect the people inside.

If the state's official position is that its agents have no obligations to protect citizens, then it would seem it is denying even the existence of a social contract. Surely, citizens cannot be expected to uphold their purported obligations if they are guaranteed nothing in return.

But perhaps these cases all happened to fall outside the purview of the state's responsibility. One could argue its obligations to provide security do not include the instances outlined in the cases above. For example, in Hartzler v. City of San Jose the plaintiff's decedent asked the police to come to her home because her ex-husband had called and threatened to kill her. The department responded that she should call them when he showed up. Unfortunately, she never got the chance because she was stabbed to death upon his arrival.

It is conceivable a contract regarding security may not obligate government officials to respond to a call unless the threat is present. But how do we know? There is no written agreement we can look to. So inevitably, the terms of the contract must be decided on in court.

Let me say that in another way. In the supposed social contract between citizens and the *government*, the terms are to be decided upon in a *government court*. If the government is a party to the dispute, there is a glaring bias, and therefore injustice in an agent of the government deciding the case.

Even if we somehow, either implicitly or explicitly, entered into an agreement, the government maintains that it has the sole right to decide what it is obligated to provide in terms of security. Practically speaking, this equates to a guarantee of injustice, as it amounts to the government unilaterally setting the terms of the so-called "agreement". A Social Contract which relies on the consent of both parties for its justification is null and void if one party has the monopoly power to set the terms.

Chapter 5

"It's The Law"

Often, objections to police misconduct, business regulations, taxation, or just some trivial statute inspire the response of "it's the law." The implication being that we shouldn't do it because the law prohibits it. This line suggests legislation is good because it is legislation, which amounts to little more than claiming might equals right.

In a practical sense, if a course of action is prohibited by law it means police or other government agents will use force or coercion to stop individuals who are observed engaging in that act. In other words, to say "it's the law" is merely pointing out overwhelming force will be used.

Logically, what is right to do does not follow from what is enforced. What is enforced is an empirical observation, how one ought to act is not. So, unless it is first shown that people should act in accordance with what is enforced, merely stating an observation does not necessarily show anyone should act in a particular way.

If the claim is rather that a law should be followed because all laws are good and just, then that is a premise that almost no one will consistently defend if they are pressed. Given the track record of laws throughout history, it is reasonable to be skeptical that any given law is just. Even if we just limit our scope to the U.S., the most obvious injustice is slavery, which was sanctioned by law. But that is just the tip of the iceberg. Racial segregation has been mandated, interracial marriage banned, sterilization[13] been forced upon promiscuous women, immigrants, the poor, and others, criticism[14] of the government banned, internment[15] forced upon people by race, the senseless killing of livestock ordered while people suffered through the Great Depression, [16] just to name a few. If history is any indication, we cannot rely on the law to tell us what is right. Each law should be evaluated based on its merit.

Government's "laws" are one thing; morality is another, and often the exact opposite. Slavish adherence to "the law" is the mark of a morally comatose person.

- Robert Higgs

Simply pointing out that "it's the law" is not enough. It is an appeal to the might of government, not the justness of the law, and the latter cannot logically follow from the former. Nor can every law be assumed to be just unless one condones the numerous questionable laws that have been enacted.

Chapter 6

The Price for Civilized Society?

"Taxes are what we pay for civilized society."

Justice Oliver Wendall Holmes

If you've ever protested that taxation is an unjust expropriation of wealth, you've likely heard the common retort "taxes are the price we pay for a civilized society." This phrase is usually attributed to Justice Holmes, and indeed, he made a similar remark in the dissent of a 1927 court case.[17] Interestingly enough, Justice Holmes' idea of a civilized society is something most Americans today would probably be horrified by. In another case[18] in 1927, for instance, Holmes penned the majority opinion which upheld the right of states to sterilize people without their consent who were categorized under the very broad label of mentally unfit. He later wrote[19] to a friend that "[E]stablishing the constitutionality of a law permitting the sterilization of imbeciles [...] gave me pleasure."

Justice Holmes is also known for his opinion in the case of Schenk v. the United States,[20] where he used the metaphor of shouting fire in a crowded theater to illustrate that some speech could be prohibited. Perhaps not as well known, is that the case involved speech which was merely in opposition to the draft. Conscription itself—forcing people to fight against their will—isn't all that civilized, but not even allowing people to protest it adds insult to injury.

The fact Justice Holmes stood for such repulsive policies does not necessarily disprove that taxes can create a civilized society or that they are necessary for any civility whatsoever. What it does illustrate, along with numerous other policies taxes have funded, is that taxes can just as well be the price we pay for mandated eugenics, involuntary servitude, the prohibition of reasonable speech, along with plenty of other uncivilized government actions. It is difficult to imagine some of the most terrible atrocities in history even occurring without a tax-funded state. After all, the Holocaust, The Holodomor,[21] and The Great Leap Forward[22] were all perpetrated by governments, and they each led to millions, even tens of millions of deaths.

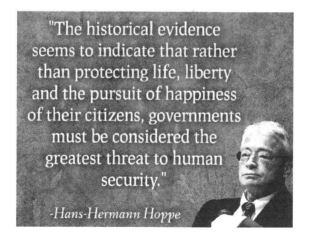

"The historical evidence seems to indicate that rather than protecting life, liberty and the pursuit of happiness of their citizens, governments must be considered the greatest threat to human security."

-Hans-Hermann Hoppe

What the claim about civilized society is getting at is that in the absence of a tax-funded state which creates order, there would be chaos and mass violence. Unlike the other arguments addressed in this book, this is not a claim about consent. Presumably, consent of the governed is irrelevant, since it is asserted that the cost of not funding a government is simply too much to bear.

The truth is the most deadly plots have been executed by governments, and a significant amount of order and relative peace are produced by non-state institutions and individuals. Furthermore, in instances of practically no government involvement, chaos has not been the norm.

If we confine our observations to present-day societies which have strong states, at the very least it can be shown that only a portion of the order and rules of society are produced by the government. The myriad non-state methods and institutions which create and alter the rules of our society often go unnoticed. Sports leagues provide their own rules and enforcement. Churches advise members on how they should regulate themselves. Firms like PayPal and eBay arbitrate disputes and provide a framework for engaging in transactions. Even security, a primary means of enforcing rules, stems from a variety of sources.

Over half[23] the world's population live in countries where privately-hired security personnel outnumber government police. In the U.S. there are over a million private security guards compared to less than 700,000 police. This tells only a fraction of the story. Practically every home and business bolster their security with locks, cameras, fences, dogs, or lights.

And of course, there are privately owned guns. It's been estimated[24] over 40% of households in America have at least one firearm. It's difficult to determine conclusively, but there may be millions of private defensive gun uses every year in the United States. Kleck and Gertz concluded[25] 2.2-2.5 million. One other way security is produced is via neighborhood watch groups. Around 40% of the U.S. population is covered by one of these programs, and there is a significant decrease[26] in crime associated with them.

We don't usually think of it in this way, but when we buy or sell products online, almost always there is some third party that has first laid down the rules. Since people appreciate a transaction experience that is streamlined, organized, and with some assurance against fraud, countless firms have jumped at the chance to provide that service. And the best part is these firms compete for customers. In other words, instead of one central government creating rules for commerce that are difficult to amend productively, many companies independently seek to give people what they want while those people can leave at any time.

A sort of anarchic order can also be observed in international trade. International business lacks an ultimate arbiter—there is no world government. Because of this, firms who wish to do business internationally tend to resolve disputes through private arbitration. Sometimes, disputes are taken to litigation in a particular country, but most of the time they are resolved without getting any government involved. According to a PricewaterhouseCoopers survey[27] of international corporations, 88% of respondents said they had used private arbitration, and "During the interviews, corporate counsel reported that more than 90% of the awards were honored by the NON-PREVAILING party. The principal reason given for compliance with the arbitral awards was to preserve a business relationship." It is not the case that these private settlements only work because there is always the threat of resorting to a government for enforcement. International firms are generally skeptical that arbitration decisions will be upheld in government courts. The researchers commented that "many corporate counsels cited countries in Africa and Central America, as well as China, India, and Russia, as states that they perceive as hostile to enforcement of foreign arbitral awards." This general lack of state enforcement has not stopped international trade, not by any means. In 2018, the total value of goods traded between China and the U.S., for example, was almost 700 billion dollars.

International law, then, represents an anarchist system of law. For the most part, legal rules are not imposed top-down by states, they are created by custom and contract between consenting parties, as well as the rulings of competing arbitration companies. Even in a modern world dominated by arguably the most centralized governments in history, there are still sectors of life that owe most if not all of their civility to non-state institutions. Taxation, if it does fund the production of SOME order, it also quite often funds disorder.

A fascinating historical example of non-state produced order is the creation[28] of the stock exchange. The first stock exchange developed in Amsterdam in the early 1600s. Government officials were highly skeptical of this new type of trading, and thus short sales, forward contracts, options, and other types of transactions were generally not enforceable in the courts. Reputation was the primary means of enforcement. A trader would need to prove his trustworthiness over time before having access to considerable trades. Similarly, private exchanges in London[29] took place under a state legal regime which outlawed various contracts. Exclusive clubs were utilized to set rules and keep out bad actors.

This is just one more example of cooperation (and civility) not relying directly on rules created and enforced by a state.

Chapter 7

Society Without the State

Perhaps your response to the preceding chapter is that non-state produced order is only possible if governments first lay down a basic set of rules and force some civility into a populace. To test this thesis, we can look at instances where there was almost no government enforcement. When similar cultures, peoples, and times are compared, societies tend to be MORE civilized when central government control is absent.

On the American western frontier, it was common for settlers to move westward faster than the government. For example, within 5 years, the population[30] of San Francisco exploded from less than 100 to over 20,000 in 1849, and only a meager police department was founded in late 1849.[31] As described[32] by historian Hubert Howe Bancroft, "The police force was small and inefficient. In case of an arrest, the law was powerless". But the people of San Francisco used alternative methods[33] to keep the peace. Private "police" (in other words, security guards) were hired by businesses and homeowners to patrol the streets to protect against crime and be on the lookout for fires. At times when crime got especially out of hand, private groups of citizens took it upon themselves to round up suspected criminals and hold trials.

Other regions of the frontier often had even less government involvement. Despite the lack of top-down force, researchers Anderson and Hill commenting[34] on the frontier between 1830 and 1900 remarked, "property rights were protected, and civil order prevailed. Private agencies provided the necessary basis for an orderly society in which property was protected and conflicts were resolved." They discuss land clubs, cattlemen's associations, and vigilance committees as just a few of the institutions which helped to facilitate order and peace.

After W. Eugene Hollon's extensive research[35] of the west, he concluded that not only was violence and oppression of minorities considerably more prevalent in the eastern American cities in the late 19th century than in the frontier communities of California and Texas, but he also strongly maintains "that the western frontier was a far more civilized, more peaceful, and safer place than American society today." Throughout his book, Hollon documents how rare, isolated incidents of bloodshed are often cited to present a gross mischaracterization of frontier life. When Hollon interviewed 1890s settlers of Oklahoma, the common theme was that frontier life was devoid of excitement. A. S. Mercer, in his studies, concluded[36] in 1894 that, "As a matter of fact there is less stealing and less lawlessness generally on the plains of the West than in any other part of the world."

There is an even more recent example which represents an opportunity to compare anarchism to statehood within the same society. Somalia is a poor society, which in the past century has had to deal with colonialism, dictatorship, and civil war. The nation-state of Somalia was formed as the British and Italian colonizers exited. Before colonization, the area was governed mostly by traditional **customary law.**[37]

This **legal system**—known as Xeer Law—is polycentric. Individuals can opt-in (usually via explicit contract) to a large "dia-paying" group which provides security, enforces restitution payments for crimes, and appoints arbiters to resolve disputes between members. Since members can change which group they belong to—and no one group has a monopoly—this represents a competitive or non-state system.

The Republic of Somalia lasted 9 years and was replaced by the dictatorship of Mohamed Siad Barre in 1969, but in 1991 Barre was **overthrown.**[38] In the years after Barre's fall, Somalia was under anarchism, and to an extent, utilization of the customary legal system **returned.**[39] Contrary to what many people might expect, however, many aspects of life for Somalis improved.

In a 2007 **study,**[40] Peter Leeson evaluated 18 economic indicators. By comparing the statehood years of 1985-1990 to the stateless years of 2000-2005, he found that 14 had improved. Also, he points out that while on paper the GDP per capita was lower under statelessness, foreign aid comprised almost 60% of GDP in the mid-80s and 100% of education was financed by foreign aid. As Leeson comments, the fall in GDP per capita, school enrollment, and literacy rate "is less a statement about the Somali government's ability to generate welfare-enhancing outcomes for its citizens than it is a reflection of foreign aid".

	1985–1990[a]	2000–2005	Welfare change
GDP per capita (PPP constant $)	836[b]	600[c,e]	?
Life expectancy (years)	46.0[b]	48.47[c,g]	Improved
One year olds fully immunized against measles (%)	30	40[h]	Improved
One year olds fully immunized against TB (%)	31	50[h]	Improved
Physicians (per 100,000)	3.4	4[h]	Improved
Infants with low birth weight (%)	16	0.3[l]	Improved
Infant mortality rate (per 1000)	152	114.89[c,g]	Improved
Maternal mortality rate (per 100,000)	1600	1100[i]	Improved
Pop. with access to water (%)	29	29[h]	Same
Pop. with access to sanitation (%)	18	26[h]	Improved
Pop. with access to at least one health facility (%)	28	54.8[k]	Improved
Extreme poverty (% < $1 per day)	60	43.2[k]	Improved
Radios (per 1000)	4.0	98.5[k]	Improved
Telephones (per 1000)	1.92[d]	14.9[k]	Improved
TVs (per 1000)	1.2	3.7[k]	Improved
Fatality due to measles	8000	5598[j,m]	Improved
Adult literacy rate (%)	24[b]	19.2[j]	Worse
Combined[n] school enrollment (%)	12.9[b]	7.5[a,f]	Worse

It should be pointed out that some of these gains were substantial. Infants with low birth weight, for example, declined by 98%, and the portion of the population with access to radios and telephones increased by 24.6 times and 7.8 times respectively.

A 2006 paper[41] also looked at Somalia under both a state and anarchy and even compared the rate of growth to neighboring countries. The authors found "that Somalia's living standards have improved generally ... not just in absolute terms, but also relative to other African countries since the collapse of the Somali central government." Relatively speaking, trade has flourished. And despite concerns that a lack of a state might translate to a lack of security, a survey[42] of pastoral traders in 1998 found that only 13% of them thought security issues were greater than in 1990.

Jamil Mubarak (1997) also found[43] that "In small communities that achieved internal law and order, their economy boomed in an unprecedented free-market environment, and the no-government situation has proven to be far better than the repressive government institutions and policies of Barré's era." Mubarak places more blame on the significant droughts that hit Somalia for its struggles than he does the loss of the central state.

One reply to these observations might be that; sure the central government in Somalia was terrible and oppressive, so anything would have been better. My response is that the type of government in a given society depends on the norms and culture of that society. Similarly, anarchism will not produce a perfect society, but relative to statehood, the results tend to be better.

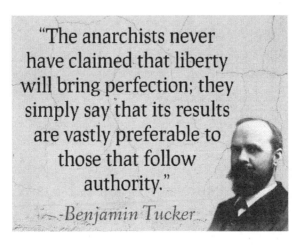

"The anarchists never have claimed that liberty will bring perfection; they simply say that its results are vastly preferable to those that follow authority."

—Benjamin Tucker

These 2 case studies disprove the claim that it is the tax-funded state that produces order and civility. A more accurate picture is that in the absence of a central state, people tend to use private, competitive, as well as cooperative institutions to help keep the peace and provide order. "Taxation is the price we pay for civilized society" is not only wrong, but it is also the opposite of the truth. Taxation is the price we pay for the disruption and weakening of order and civility.

Chapter 8

Conclusion

The validity of the notion of a social contract is crucial for political questions. It should inform our judgment of the justness as well as consequences of state power and authority. For the most common justifications for state authority, these arguments fail.

From the outset, any kind of general understanding of what the social contract entails is out the window. People do not even offer similar theories for why the state's authority is justified. At most, one could perhaps argue most people have a vague idea that there is some nebulous social contract.

Some arguments rely on the state owning huge tracts of land, but a coherent theory for why this is needs to overcome the historical reality of conquest. When assertions are made that you should leave if you dislike the government's rules, there is either an implicit claim of ownership or jurisdiction, which has yet to be shown.

Arguments which attempt to show consent as the basis for authority fail because they either depend on a constitution (which isn't based on consent) or take some action (or non-action) as implied consent. As we have seen, there is not a direct connection between actions and government services and rules, and politicians who

claim to represent their constituency make a mockery of
"representation". While citizens are forced to keep up
their end of the "contract", government agents are not.
Supreme Court justices have gone as far as
recommending citizens should hire private security if
they want protection.

Nor can the mere fact that there is law be a valid reason
that it is justified. That claim suffers from a logical
fallacy. Not to mention, it would justify all manner of
terrible actions. Moreover, the upkeep of a central state
via taxation is not what makes societies civilized. Order
stems from numerous sources, and even when the state
is completely removed from the picture, people thrive.

I hope my arguments and evidence have been enough to
persuade you that the state as an institution is not a
legitimate organization. It sows disorder, violates
consent on a massive scale, and rips off its citizens.
Alternatively, perhaps I have given you intellectual
ammunition against the government's apologists. Either
way, thank you for reading my book. Best of luck as you
make your way in a world dominated by unjust
institutions.

Notes

[1] Wood, Robert W. "U.S. Has World's Highest Fee To Renounce Citizenship." Forbes, Forbes Magazine, 2015, www.forbes.com/sites/robertwood/2015/10/23/u-s-has-worlds-highest-fee-to-renounce-citizenship/.

[2] Ashman, Joshua, and Ephraim Moss. "Note to Expats: No, You Didn't Dodge the U.S. Tax Bullet." Money, 2016, money.com/money/4298634/expat-expatriate-taxes-us-myths/.

[3] Martinez, Andreas Kohl. "Why Liechtenstein Works." Jacobite, 2017, jacobitemag.com/2017/08/04/why-liechtenstein-works-self-determination-and-market-governance/.

[4] "Who Owns Antarctica?" Australian Government, Department of the Environment and Energy, Australian Antarctic Division, 2017, www.antarctica.gov.au/about-antarctica/people-in-antarctica/who-owns-antarctica.

[5] "Overview - Convention & Related Agreements." United Nations, United Nations, 2019, www.un.org/depts/los/convention_agreements/convention_overview_convention.htm.

[6] Kratz, Jessie. "'Rogue Island': The Last State to Ratify the Constitution." National Archives and Records Administration, National Archives and Records Administration, 2015, prologue.blogs.archives.gov/2015/05/18/rogue-island-the-last-state-to-ratify-the-constitution/.

[7] Warren v. District of Columbia (444 A.2d. 1, D.C. Ct. of Ap. 1981)

[8] Hartzler v. City of San Jose 46 Cal.App.3d 6 (1975)

[9] Castle Rock v. Gonzales, 545 U.S. 748 (2005)

[10] DeShaney v. Winnebago County, 489 U.S. 189 (1989)

[11] Fleshler, David. "Broward Sheriff's Sergeant Called 'an Absolute, Total Failure' as Parkland Shooting Panel Slams Agency." Sun Sentinel, South Florida Sun-Sentinel, 2018, www.sun-sentinel.com/local/broward/parkland/florida-school-shooting/fl-ne-florida-school-shooting-commission-day-2-story.html.

[12] Huriash, Lisa J. "Cops and Schools Had No Duty to Shield Students in Parkland Shooting, Says Judge Who Tossed Lawsuit." Sun Sentinel, South Florida Sun-Sentinel, 2018, www.sun-sentinel.com/local/broward/parkland/florida-school-shooting/fl-ne-douglas-survivor-lawsuit-federal-judge-20181217-story.html.

[13] Ko, Lisa. "Unwanted Sterilization and Eugenics Programs in the United States." PBS, Public Broadcasting Service, 2016, www.pbs.org/independentlens/blog/unwanted-sterilization-and-eugenics-programs-in-the-united-states/.

[14] "U.S. Congress Passes Sedition Act." History.com, A&E Television Networks, 5 Nov. 2009, www.history.com/this-day-in-history/u-s-congress-passes-sedition-act.

[15] Weik, Taylor. "Behind Barbed Wire: Remembering America's Largest Internment Camp." NBCNews.com, NBCUniversal News Group, 2016, www.nbcnews.com/news/asian-america/behind-barbed-wire-remembering-america-s-largest-internment-camp-n535086.

[16] "Culling the Herds." Living History Farm, livinghistoryfarm.org/farminginthe30s/crops_17.html.

[17] Compania General de Filipinas v. Collector :: 279 U.S. 306 (1929)

[18] Buck v. Bell 274 U.S. 200 (1927)

[19] Alschuler, Albert W. Law without Values: the Life, Work, and Legacy of Justice Holmes. University of Chicago Press, 2002.

[20] Schenck v. United States 249 U.S. 47 (1919)

[21] Kiger, Patrick J. "How Joseph Stalin Starved Millions in the Ukrainian Famine." History.com, A&E Television Networks, 2019, www.history.com/news/ukrainian-famine-stalin.

[22] "Great Leap Forward." Encyclopædia Britannica, Encyclopædia Britannica, Inc., 1998, www.britannica.com/event/Great-Leap-Forward.

[23] McCarthy, Niall. "Where Private Security Outnumbers The Police." Statista Infographics, 2017, www.statista.com/chart/10925/where-private-security-outnumbers-the-police/.

[24] "Firearms in the U.S." Www.statista.com, 2019, www.statista.com/topics/1287/firearms-in-the-us/.

[25] Gary Kleck and Marc Gertz, Armed Resistance to Crime: The Prevalence and Nature of Self-Defense with a Gun, 86 J. Crim. L. & Criminology 150 (1995). https://scholarlycommons.law.northwestern.edu/jclc/vol86/iss1/8

[26] Wihbey, John. "U.S. Justice Department: Does Neighborhood Watch Reduce Crime?" Journalist's Resource, 2012, journalistsresource.org/studies/government/criminal-justice/us-justice-department-neighborhood-watch-reduce-crime/.

[27] PriceWaterhouseCoopers. 2008. "International Arbitration: Corporate Attitudes and Practices." London

[28] Stringham, Edward Peter, The Extralegal Development of Securities Trading in Seventeenth Century Amsterdam (December 18, 2001). Quarterly Review of Economics and Finance, Vol. 43, No. 2, p. 321, 2003. Available at SSRN: https://ssrn.com/abstract=1676251

[29] Stringham, Edward Peter, The Emergence of the London Stock Exchange as a Self-Policing Club (2002). Journal of Private Enterprise, Vol. 17, No. 2, pp. 1-19, Spring 2002. Available at SSRN: https://ssrn.com/abstract=1676253

[30] "San Francisco Population." San Francisco History, 2018, www.sfgenealogy.org/sf/history/hgpop.htm.

[31] Ackerson, Sherman, et al. "SFPD History." SFPD: SFPD History, 2019, web.archive.org/web/20070807095555/http:/www.sfgov.org/site/police_index.asp?id=20204.

[32] Bancroft, Hubert Howe. 1887. History of the Pacific States of North America: Popular Tribunals. San Francisco: History Company.

[33] Stringham, Edward. "San Francisco's Private Police Force." Reason.com, Reason, 2015, reason.com/2015/07/21/san-franciscos-private-police/.

[34] Anderson, Terry, and P.J. Hill. "The Not So Wild, Wild West." Mises Institute, 2010, mises.org/library/not-so-wild-wild-west.

[35] Hollon, William Eugene. Frontier Violence Another Look. Oxford University Press, 1976.

[36] Mercer, A. S. The Banditti of the Plains. University of Oklahoma Press, 1954.

[37] "Somali Law." Legal Systems Very Different From Ours, by David D. Friedman et al., Publisher Not Identified, 2019.

[38] Janzen, Jörg H.A., and Loan M. Lewis. "Somalia." Encyclopædia Britannica, Encyclopædia Britannica, Inc., 2019, www.britannica.com/place/Somalia.

[39] "Somali Law." Legal Systems Very Different From Ours, by David D. Friedman et al., Publisher Not Identified, 2019.

[40] Leeson, Peter T., Better Off Stateless: Somalia Before and after Government Collapse. Journal of Comparative Economics, Vol. 35, No. 4, 2007. Available at SSRN: https://ssrn.com/abstract=879798

[41] Powell, B., R. Ford, and A. Nowrasteh. 2008. "Somalia after State Collapse: Chaos or Improvement?" Journal of Economic Behavior and Organization 67 (3–4): 657–670.
[42] "Somalia: Economy Without State." Somalia: Economy Without State, by Peter D. Little, James Currey, 2003, p. 125.
[43] Mubarak, Jamil A., 1997. "The "hidden hand" behind the resilience of the stateless economy of Somalia," World Development, Elsevier, vol. 25(12), pages 2027-2041, December.

Made in the USA
Coppell, TX
21 February 2021

50584869R00024